CHRISTMAS

Its History and Meaning

James A. Fowler

C.I.Y. PUBLISHING
P.O. BOX 1822
FALLBROOK, CALIFORNIA 92088-1822

www.christinyou.net

CHRISTMAS
Its History and Meaning

Second Edition

Published by
C.I.Y. PUBLISHING
P.O. BOX 1822
FALLBROOK, CALIFORNIA 92088-1822

ISBN 978-1-929541-05-8

Scripture quotations are from the New American Standard Bible, Copyright © 1960, 1962, 1963, 1968, 1971, 1972, 1973, 1975 by The Lockman Foundation, LaHabra, California.

Printed in the United States of America

ACKNOWLEDGEMENTS

The participants of the Neighborhood Church of San Diego County, located in Fallbrook, California, must be acknowledged as the first to hear and respond to these messages when they were first delivered during the Advent season of 1998. They are a loving fellowship of Christians who truly know the personal meaning of Christmas.

Acknowledgement must also be made of the assistance given to me by my sister (both biological and spiritual), Sylvia Burnett, who brought this book to fruition by editing the text and formatting the pagination for this revised edition. Without her efforts this book may never have materialized, and certainly not in such an aesthetically pleasing form as she has prepared.

Jim Fowler
September, 2006

Table of Contents

INTRODUCTION

Reference to "Christmas" brings such varying images to people's minds around the world. Many in the Western world of the northern hemisphere think of a winter holiday that often involves snow and evergreen trees, but those closer to the equator and in the southern hemisphere of our planet think of a holiday that occurs in the warm climate of summer.

In addition to the climate factors, there are a multitude of varying cultural customs that are associated with the Christmas holiday in the diverse regions and countries of the world. Developed through the centuries of almost two millennia, the origins of many of these customs often cannot be historically ascertained.

Though recognized as having its origin in Christian remembrance of the birth of Jesus, the Christmas holiday has often become enculturated as a season of good cheer, merriment, and gift-giving enjoyed by the majority of people regardless of religion, as they participate in a governmentally declared holiday.

Yet, among Christian peoples there is still disagreement concerning the legitimacy and desirability of participating in the celebration of the Christmas holiday.

Amidst all this diversity of thought about Christmas, it should be instructive to review the history and meaning of Christmas. This small book will consider:

(1) the foundational history of the birth of Jesus,

(2) the formulated theological explanation of the incarnation for the Christian faith,

(3) some of the origins and meanings of the traditions that have developed in the celebration of Christmas, and

(4) the importance of personal participation in the dynamic of God's presence in our lives.

Chapter 1

CHRISTMAS
Considered Historically

Technically, it is not "Christmas" that we are considering in this chapter, but the historical birth or advent of Jesus Christ as recorded in the natal narratives of Jesus in the two gospels of Matthew and Luke (Matt. 1:18–2:23; Luke 1:26-56; 2:1-40). The celebration of the birth of Jesus was later referred to in the English-speaking world as "Christmas."

TWELVE EVENTS OF JESUS' BIRTH

A popular Christmas song refers to cultural gift-giving on the "Twelve Days of Christmas," but we shall consider the twelve basic events of the historical birth of Jesus as recorded in the gospel narratives of Matthew and Luke.

(1) Joseph and Mary betrothed —
Matt. 1:18,19; Luke 1:26,27

According to the accepted Jewish betrothal custom, Joseph and Mary had made a contractual pledge to be married. This commitment was considered so binding that dissolution required a formal decree of divorce. Cohabitation and sexual coitus were not considered proper during the betrothal period as the betrothed parties were preparing for their wedding festival.

Tradition indicates that Joseph was considerably older than Mary. The absence of later mention of Joseph may indicate that he died while Jesus was fairly young, and was not alive during the time of Jesus' passion.

We do know that Joseph was a carpenter (Matt. 13:55), and that he seemed to be able to care for his family, even in a foreign country (Egypt).

For a betrothed woman to become pregnant was a disgrace. Joseph's knowledge that he had not had intercourse with Mary would have given him cause to dissolve the betrothal, as he considered doing; but being a righteous and merciful man, he was willing to do so without public humiliation.

The supernatural conception of Jesus in the womb of Mary was caused or created by the Holy Spirit. As the "second Adam," Jesus was only the second man to ever live who had only God as His father. His was a divine paternity. Though fully human, "born of a woman" (Gal. 4:4), He did not participate in the sin consequences predicated to all of the human race because of Adam's sin (Rom. 5:12-21).

(2) Angel appears to Mary — Luke 1:26-38

Tradition has indicated that Mary was quite young at the time of her betrothal and pregnancy. It is often estimated that she was between twelve and sixteen years of age, though there is no biblical evidence concerning her age.

Mary's statement in the Magnificat (Luke 1:46-55) has been taken by some to indicate that she was of "low-estate" (Luke 1:48) socially. These words may simply indicate her humility at being so used of God.

Befuddled at the announcement that she would bear a child though she had not had sexual intercourse with any man (cf. vs. 34), she was nonetheless willing to accept the explanation of the angelic messenger that "nothing will be impossible with God" (vs. 37). She consented to be so used of God in accord with His declaration.

Later in history Mary was elevated in veneration in the Roman Catholic Church. The Council of Ephesus (431 A.D.) referred to her as the "Mother of God" (*theotokos*). She was regarded as immaculately conceived without sinful depravity, a perpetual virgin never having had sexual contact with any man (cf. Matt. 13:57; Mark 6:4; John 7:5), taken up to heaven in an assumption of body and soul, and the "queen of heaven" who served as a co-mediator (cf. I Tim. 2:5) and co-redemptrix with Jesus.

(3) Angel appears to Joseph — Matt. 1:20-25

Joseph was likewise informed by an angel that the conception of the child in Mary's womb was effected by the Holy Spirit. Joseph must have been a man full of trust in God.

Joseph was told that he was to name the son "Jesus," as Mary had been told also (Luke 1:31). The name "Jesus" comes from the Hebrew *Yeshua*, derived from *Yehoshua*, meaning "Yahweh is salvation." It is the same name as "Joshua" in the Hebrew Old Testament. In further amplification of the meaning of His name, Joseph was told that Jesus "will save His people (those identified with Him) from their sins" (vs. 21), as a savior (cf. Luke 2:11; John 4:42).

Citing the prophet Isaiah, the angel informed Joseph that this child would be the fulfillment of the prophecy of "the virgin bearing a son, and calling His name 'Immanuel,' meaning 'God with us' " (Isa. 7:14).

(4) Roman census ordered — Luke 2:1-6

History records that Caesar Augustus made a decree in 8 B.C. to enact a census of the Roman Empire. Herod the Great, king over the Palestinian region under the authority of Rome, would have been responsible for implementing the census in his jurisdiction. Apparently he determined that this was best facilitated by having the Jewish people go back to their familial cities for registration and identification.

Joseph was from the house and family of David, whose familial city was Bethlehem in Judea, approximately five miles south of Jerusalem. A particular date must have been set or else Joseph would not have felt compelled to take his pregnant bride on such an arduous journey of almost 70 miles from Nazareth to Bethlehem.

(5) Child born to Mary in Bethlehem — Luke 2:7

Arriving in Bethlehem and unable to find lodging due to the influx of visitors arriving for census registration, Joseph and Mary were forced to spend the night in a cave or grotto where the travelers' animals were stabled. That night she gave birth to a son.

Few details are provided concerning the birth, and whether Mary had any assistance other than her husband. Apparently it was a natural birth-delivery

8

following a nine-month gestation period. It is referred to as a "virgin birth" only because Mary had never had sexual relations with Joseph or any other man, conceiving a child only by the Holy Spirit.

(6) Shepherds come to the stable — Luke 2:8-20

Shepherds in the region of Bethlehem were tending their flocks at night. Perhaps it was lambing season. Some have conjectured that these were "lambs without blemish" being prepared for sacrifices at the temple in Jerusalem. In the Palestinian social milieu of that time, shepherds were regarded as a low-class subculture and were often isolated from the mainstream of Jewish life. How appropriate that Jesus' birth was first announced to the lowly and outcast.

The supernatural phenomenon of angels played a big role in the story of Jesus' birth, as they appeared to Mary, Joseph, and the shepherds. A multitude of angels appeared to the shepherds, praising God and announcing God's peace among men (cf. Isa. 9:6).

(7) The Child is circumcised and given the name of "Jesus" — Luke 2:21

When Jesus was eight days old, He was circumcised according to Jewish custom, probably in Bethlehem. This was a distinctive physical mark given to all Jewish males from the time of Abraham (Gen. 17:9-14).

It was also at this time that Jesus was officially given the name "Jesus," as Joseph and Mary had both been instructed (cf. Matt. 1:21; Luke 1:31).

(8) Jesus presented at temple when 40 days old — Luke 2:22-40

"Born of a woman, under the Law" (Gal. 4:4), partaking of Jewish ethnicity and heritage, Jesus participated in the traditional Jewish rites of religion, including circumcision and presentation at the temple in Jerusalem. Levitical Law required 33 days of purification for a woman who had born a son (Lev. 12:4) before she could go to the temple. These days were probably spent in Bethlehem with the newborn infant, Jesus.

After the required time and in accord with the Law (Exod. 13:2,12), Joseph and Mary took Jesus to the temple and made a sacrificial offering, "a pair of turtledoves or two young pigeons," which was the offering for those unable to afford a lamb for sacrifice (Lev. 12:8).

Simeon, a righteous and devout old Jewish man, had been told by God that he would not die until he had seen the expected Messiah. When Jesus was presented in the temple, Simeon declared that he had seen God's salvation who would be "a light of revelation to the Gentiles" (Isa. 42:6; 49:6) and not only to Jews. Simeon told Mary that her son would be the basis of many Jewish people either stumbling or being resurrected (vs. 34), but this would require the piercing suffering of her own soul (apparently alluding to the death of Jesus). Anna, a prophetess in the temple, also recognized the infant Jesus as God's Redeemer (vs. 38).

Having performed the requirements of the Jewish Law, Joseph took Mary and Jesus back to reside in Nazareth (vs. 39).

(9) Magi from the East seek and find Jesus —
Matt. 2:1-12

Though a popular Christmas carol refers to "three kings of the orient," the Bible never indicates that there were three magi or that they were kings. In fact, a distinction of "king" and "magi" is made in Matthew 2:1.

The term "magi" comes from the same root as "magic" and "magicians." These persons were probably astrological magicians or sorcerers from Persia, Babylon or Arabia. Such persons (cf. Dan. 2:2) watched the stars, were able to predict solar and lunar eclipses, and attempted to predict events to come. Their abilities often gave them audience to the courts of kings, as well as great sway over the people. It should also be noted that in the eastern religion of Zoroastrianism there was the expectation of a coming king who would be announced by a sign in the sky.

That the magi have been calculated as three in number is undoubtedly a conjecture based on the three different kinds of gifts mentioned. Their gifts were gold, frankincense (fragrant gum resin used as incense), and myrrh (aromatic resin used in perfumes). The costly nature of these gifts provides a contrast that evidences the universality of Jesus Christ: the shepherds were poor, local and Jewish, while the magi were rich, foreign and Gentile. Jesus came for all men, both Jew and Gentile (cf. Acts 1:8; Eph. 2:11-18).

The star that the magi observed has been the source of much conjecture and astronomical calculation. Was it an astronomical occurrence such as a meteor, or a comet, or a nova? It is calculated that Halley's comet would have appeared in 11 B.C. Or was the star seen by the magi a divinely placed, supernatural light in the sky?

It must also be asked whether anyone other than the magi saw this star. Since they are the only ones reported to have seen the star, it might have been a special revelation for them. Herod inquired of them when and where they had first seen the star (vs. 7), so apparently it was not a phenomenon of sufficient import that others had noticed.

We must remember that just because the magi saw a bright star in the heavens, it is not likely that they would just climb aboard a camel and make tracks in the desert. A caravan would have to be prepared, and supplies would have to be purchased. Probably a considerable group of servants would have to be assembled, along with beasts of burden, and perhaps even soldiers to fight off highway bandits. This might have been an impressive entourage. Perhaps this explains why Herod "was troubled, and all Jerusalem with him" (Matt. 2:3).

The request of the magi for "the King of the Jews" (Matt. 2:2) would have been particularly troubling to Herod. The Jews did not have their own king (though they desired such), and Herod had been declared king over the Palestinian region where the Jewish peoples lived.

The star did not necessarily guide the magi to Palestine, though the popular song refers to "following yonder star." If the magi were led by the star, why did they stop in Jerusalem to inquire where the King could be found? Why did it not guide them to Bethlehem? Perhaps it was a singular celestial phenomenon.

When the magi asked where "the King of the Jews" could be found, Herod interrogated the Sanhedrin, the Jewish council of "chief priests and

scribes," to ascertain where the Messianic King was to be born. They advised him that prophecy indicated that it was in "Bethlehem, in the land of Judea" (Micah 5:2). The city of Bethlehem, located five miles south of Jerusalem, was the familial city of famed King David
(I Sam. 16:4; 17:12). God told David that his descendant would be the Messianic King (II Sam. 7:12,13).

The star that the magi had previously seen reappeared, and they were elated at its reappearance. The celestial light appears to have led them in a different direction than Bethlehem, to which Herod had directed them (Matt. 2:8). Perhaps the star directed them to Nazareth where Joseph, Mary and Jesus had gone to live after Jesus' presentation in the temple (Luke 2:39).

The time required for the magi to journey to Palestine was probably many months, and possibly more than a year. Matthew records that the magi entered into a "house" (Matt. 2:11) rather than a stable. Though Jesus is referred to as an infant "babe" (Greek *brephos*) while in Bethlehem (Luke

2:12,16), He is referred to as a "young child" (Greek *paidon*) when the magi arrive (Matt. 2:8,9,11).

(10) Joseph and Mary take Jesus and flee to Egypt — Matt. 2:13-15

An angel advised Joseph to take Mary and the Child, Jesus, to Egypt to avoid Herod's search for Him. Matthew regarded this action as a fulfillment of Hosea's prophecy of God's delivering His Son out of Egypt (Hosea 11:1).

(11) Herod orders massacre of male children — Matt. 2:16-18

Herod had been appointed by Caesar Augustus in 40 B.C. to serve as Palestine's ruler under Roman authority. Herod was respected by the Romans as a builder of fortresses, cities, temples, aqueducts. He encouraged foreign trade by building a port at Caesarea. He was an accomplished political conciliator who forced religious and ethnic groups to cooperate.

The Jews, on the other hand, hated Herod for his heavy taxation, for his tyrannous cruelty and selfishness, and for his political scheming which included many murders.

When the magi did not return from Bethlehem with a report as Herod had requested (Matt. 2:8), and that probably because they never went to Bethlehem, Herod concluded that he had been outwitted, and he became enraged. Herod ordered his soldiers to slay all children under two years of age. He chose this age group because he knew the child was no longer a newborn infant, but must have been between one and two years of age. This calculation was probably based on the time when the magi said they first saw the star, and the time required for their travel to Palestine.

The slaughter of the Jewish infants is regarded by Matthew as being the fulfillment of Jeremiah's prophecy of "great mourning and weeping for the children" (Jere. 31:15), which leads into his prophecy of a new covenant (Jere. 31:21-34).

(12) Return to Nazareth after Herod's death —
Matt. 2:19-23

When Herod was dead, an angel again appeared to Joseph advising him to take Mary and Jesus back to the land of Israel. Hearing that Herod's son, Archelaus, was ruling in Judea, and being warned in a dream not to go there, Joseph took his family back to Nazareth in Galilee.

THE DATING OF JESUS' BIRTH

Our present calendar method of dating was first established in the sixth century (533 A.D.) by Dionysius Exiguus. He was a monk who was commissioned by Pope John I to develop a calendar system other than the old Roman calendar, which dated years as AUC
(*ab urbe condita*) from the founding of the city of Rome. Dionysius determined that historical time should be made to pivot at the birth of Jesus, the singular most important event in history. Using the best historical sources available to him at the time, Dionysius calculated the years back to Jesus' birth

and established the first year of Jesus' life as 1 A.D. (*anno Domini*), meaning "year of the Lord." Years prior to the birth of Jesus were calculated backwards beginning with 1 B.C. (before Christ).

Later it was determined on the basis of additional historical evidence that Dionysius had miscalculated by several years. How did this happen? Dionysius found a statement by Clement of Alexandria that Jesus was born in the twenty-eighth year of the reign of Emperor Augustus. What he failed to take into account was that Augustus first ruled under his given name of Octavian before the Roman Senate conferred on him the name of Caesar Augustus. Scholars now conclude that King Herod probably died in the year 4 B.C.

What, then, are the criteria by which we might attempt to determine the date of Jesus' birth? Correlating the biblical records with known historical dates, the following observations can be made:

(1) Herod the Great ruled as king in Judea from 40 B.C. to 4 B.C. Allowing time for the magi to travel to Palestine, and noting that Herod sought to kill all

infants up to two years of age, we must allow at least two years prior to 4 B.C. for the birth of Jesus.

(2) Caesar Augustus had ordered a census (Luke 2:1). Historical records seem to indicate that Augustus Caesar ordered censuses in 28 B.C., 8 B.C., and 14 A.D. If the census of 8 B.C. is the one referred to in scripture, we must allow time for the logistical implementation of the census in regards to census-takers, notification, etc.

(3) That Quirinius was governor in Syria (Luke 2:2) when a census was ordered has often been used to discount the scripture record, because Varus was the governor of record in Syria beginning in 7 B.C. An inscription was discovered by archaeologists in 1764 which seems to indicate that Quirinius may have had an official capacity in Syria both in the years B.C. and A.D. This is not much help in dating the birth of Jesus.

(4) Luke, a very trustworthy historian, records that Jesus began His ministry when He was "about thirty years of age" (Luke 3:23). Granted, the word "about" allows for approximation.

(5) John records that soon after the commencement of Jesus' ministry when Jesus first

cleansed the temple, the Jewish authorities indicated that Herod's rebuilding of the temple was in its forty-sixth year (John 2:20). Historical records indicate that the temple construction began in 22 B.C., making the forty-sixth year of construction about 24 A.D. Thirty years prior to 24 A.D. would be approximately 6 B.C., which references well with the above noted criteria, though no certainty of His birth year can be assigned.

The time of year, i.e., the month and day of Jesus' birth, are even more questionable. Herod would have likely implemented Augustus Caesar's edict for a census in such a way as to best facilitate such for the Palestinian people. He certainly did so in accord with the Jewish nationalistic model of "returning to one's own family city of origin," which was not the procedure followed in the rest of the Roman Empire. The census would probably not have been ordered at a time that would have interfered with spring and summer agricultural operations, which were so important to the Palestinian economy. Therefore, the date of the census was probably not in wintertime (November to March) when Palestine can be very cold and travel can be very difficult. The fact that the shepherds were tending their sheep at night might indicate warmer temperatures, particularly the spring season when the lambs were generally born. But since the spring was the time of preparation for agricultural planting, perhaps the fall season after the harvest would have been most convenient. We do not know the season when Herod ordered the census to be taken. It was apparently a definite, specific time, or else Joseph would not have taken Mary on such a trip of approximately 70 miles so close to the time of her delivery.

Speculations concerning the dating of Jesus' birth have abounded in Christian history. Clement of Alexandria (c. 150-220 A.D.) dated the birth of Christ on November 18, but noted there was great variance of opinion about the date of Christ's birth. An early anonymous work, *de Pascha Computus* (The Computation of the Passion), indicated March 28 as the day of Christ's birth. Others (for example, Julius Africanus, 221 A.D.) regarded March 25 as the birth date. Many of these conjectures were based on the premise of a perfect annual period between Jesus' birth and death. Calculating from His death in the spring at Passover time, usually calculated as March 25 or April 6, they thus selected the same date for His birth. Gradually this became identified with the date of the supernatural conception of Jesus, and the date of His birth was pushed back nine months to December 25 or January 6. Augustine (354-430 A.D.), in his work *De Trinitate*, for example, writes that "He is believed to have been conceived on the 25th of March, upon which day also He suffered; . . . and He was born according to tradition on December 25th."

Others have indicated that December 25th was selected as the day of Jesus' birth because it was the time of the winter *solstice* when light overcomes darkness. The Egyptian calendar long celebrated May 20 as the date of the entry of Jesus and His parents into Egypt as they fled from Herod, but this does not facilitate the dating of Jesus' birth because we do not know how much time elapsed between His birth and the family's flight. The month and day of Jesus' birth must be left as uncertain.

Despite the lack of definite dating of Jesus' birth, the historical event of His birth is most important to the Christian faith. Christianity is not the perpetuation of merely subjective phenomena, but is founded on verifiable historical events. Those who would question the historicity of Jesus and identify the records of His life as but religious myth are either uninformed or have an agenda to deny the truth. F.F. Bruce has written:

> Some writers may toy with the fancy of a "Christ-myth," but they do not do so on the ground of historical evidence. The historicity of Christ is as axiomatic for an unbiased historian as the historicity of Julius Caesar. It is not historians who propagate the "Christ-myth" theories.[1]

The witness of the Jewish historian Josephus, who lived in the latter part of the first century (c. 37-100 A.D.), is particularly pertinent. Writing of the time when Pilate was procurator, Josephus notes,

Now, there was about this time Jesus, a wise man, if it be lawful to call him a man, for he was a doer of wonderful works — a teacher of such men as receive the truth with pleasure. He drew over to him both many of the Jews, and many of the Gentiles. He was the Christ; and when Pilate, at the suggestion of the principal men amongst us, had condemned him to the cross, those that loved him at the first did not forsake him, for he appeared to them alive again the third day, as the divine prophets had foretold these and ten thousand other wonderful things concerning him; and the tribe of Christians, so named from him, are not extinct at this day.₂

The historical verification of Jesus' life is well attested. Though the date of Jesus' birth is unknown, the fact of His birth is well authenticated.

Millions of men have been born, lived and died throughout the history of mankind. What, then, makes the birth of this child different than all others, many of whom have been forgotten or are merely names on genealogical records? The birthdates of a few great personages are remembered (example: George Washington, Abraham Lincoln, Martin

Luther King, etc.), but for the most part, people soon forget historical trivia about the lives of their forebears. Obviously, the birth of Jesus, from which most of the world determines historical, calendar time (though miscalculated), has had an impact beyond all others. We must go beyond the historical details of His birth to an explanation of this singularly significant event.

Chapter 2

CHRISTMAS
Considered Theologically

The historical event of an infant's birth in
Bethlehem in approximately 6 B.C. was but the
external and physical expression of a singular and
never-to-be-repeated divine action. The theological
implications of what transpired on that night must
be explored in order to understand the divine reality
of the event.

Although Jesus was undoubtedly regarded by
most of His contemporaries in Palestine as but the
physical "son of Joseph" (Luke 2:48; 3:23; 4:22; John
1:45; 6:42), the divine factors of His birth and Being
could only be recognized by divine revelation. The
recognition that Jesus was God as well as man could
not be surmised by "flesh and blood," human

27

reasoning, but only by the revelation of His Father in heaven (Matt. 16:17).

Even prior to His physical birth the prophets indicated that the expected Messiah would be God expressed in humanity. Through Isaiah, God told Ahaz that "a virgin will be with child and bear a son, and she will call His name Immanuel" (Isa. 7:14), which Matthew explains, means "God with us" or "God in us" (Matt. 1:23). Later Isaiah explained that "a child will be born to us, a son will be given to us; . . . and His name will be called Wonderful Counselor, Mighty God, Eternal Father, Prince of Peace" (Isa. 9:6), names which evidence the deity of the expected Messianic child.

Angels informed both Mary and Joseph that the child she would bear should be named "Jesus" (Matt. 1:21; Luke 1:31), which means "Jehovah saves," as it would be He (Jehovah in this male child) Who would save His people from their sins (Matt. 1:21), as only God can do. In addition, the angel told Mary that the child would be "the Son of the Most High" (Luke 1:32), and that "the holy offspring shall be called the Son of God" (Luke 1:35). The angels announced to the shepherds outside

28

Bethlehem that the child who had been born was "a Savior, Christ the Lord" (Luke 2:11), which would be understood to mean "the Messianic Savior, Yahweh personified."

Christmas can only be understood theologically as the singular divine event that it was if we recognize that the eternal and infinite God intervened and took action to intersect with man in the space/time context of human history in order to invest Himself in a human creature for the purpose of assuming the consequences of sin and restoring humanity to its divinely intended function. The God of the universe voluntarily took the initiative of acting in His grace to condescend and "come down from heaven" (John 3:13; 6:33,38,42) in the Son in order to meet man where he was, on earth in his fallen, sinful condition, becoming a man Himself to bear the death consequences of sin, which only a man could bear, since God cannot die.

THE PRE-EXISTENCE OF THE SON

A theological consideration of Christmas must commence with an understanding that the Son of

God was existent prior to His being born as a baby in Bethlehem and being given the name "Jesus." The Son existed eternally in the Trinitarian oneness of the Godhead. As "eternal God," and remaining so when He became a child (cf. Isa. 9:6), He was and is immutably and unchangeably divine. Becoming a man could in no way alter His deity.

The two issues that must be addressed in considering the pre-existence of the Son are His eternal existence and His eternal deity, which are so inextricably united as to be incapable of separation, but we shall attempt to do so for the purpose of explanation.

Through the prophet Micah, the Lord declared, "From you [Bethlehem] One will go forth for Me to be ruler in Israel. His goings forth are from long ago, from the days of eternity" (Micah 5:2). John perceived in his revelation that Jesus is "the One Who is and Who was and Who is to come" (Rev. 1:8) — eternally existent, and eternally immutable in that eternal existence, for "Jesus is the same yesterday, and today and forever" (Heb. 13:8). "He is before all things" (Col. 1:17), declared Paul. "He was in the beginning with God. All things came into being by

Him; and apart from Him nothing came into being that has come into being" (John 1:2,3), John states in the prologue of his gospel, noting that John the Baptist asserted that "He existed before me" (John 1:15), even though Jesus was born six months after John. Jesus Himself asserted that "before Abraham was" (John 8:58), He existed as the "I AM" of the eternally present existence of Yahweh (cf. Exod. 3:14). Prior to His manifestation as a man, the Son "was before" (John 6:62) in heaven, eternally existent as God.

Some have questioned the eternal existence of the Son as God, citing some New Testament passages which can be misinterpreted to imply that Jesus had a beginning as a created being. The apostle John, for example, refers to Jesus as "the only begotten Son" (John 1:14,18; 3:16,18; I John 4:9) of God. The Greek word that John employs, *monogenes*, does not necessarily refer to a derivatively created being, but to the unique, one-of-a-kind, familial consubstantiality that the divine Son shared with the Father God. Likewise, Paul's reference to Jesus as the "first-born over all creation" (Col. 1:15), using the Greek word *prototokos*, does not necessarily refer to the "first-created," but to the preeminent and supreme One over all creation, for he goes on to explain that "by Him all things were created" (Col. 1:16). These verses do not challenge or negate the previously cited verses which affirm the eternal pre-existence of the Son, as God.

The eternal deity of the Son implied by His eternal existence is also expressed in the prologue of John's gospel, where he writes, "In the beginning was the Word, and the Word was with God, and the Word was God. He was in the beginning with God" (John 1:1,2). Despite misguided interpretive attempts to supply an indirect article in order to imply that "the Word was *a* god," the only valid exegesis of the text recognizes that "the Word was God." The Word, the expressive agency of God, became flesh (John 1:14) in the Person of Jesus.

In the Christological explanation that Paul wrote to the Philippians, he explained that "although He existed in the form of God, He did not regard equality with God a thing to be grasped" (Phil. 2:6). The Son pre-existed as God. That Paul refers to His "existing in the form (*morphe*) of God," does not imply a phantasmal illusion, an exact replica, or a secondary configuration, as some have suggested, but indicates that the Son existed as the very essence of God's Being, functioning in the enactment and expression of that Being by independent prerogative. As the very Being of God, He acted as God. Recognizing His eternal equality with God, ontologically in His Being and operationally in His functional action, and recognizing that such eternal equality was immutable so that He was incapable of being less than God, the Son did not regard such equality a thing to be "grasped, held on to, or possessively maintained." The Son of God did not have to demand an "equal rights amendment" to assert, protect, or preserve His equality and oneness of Being and function as God. Rather, He was voluntarily willing to take the form of a man, knowing that while functioning as a man He would never be less than God.

———— ❧ ————

If Jesus did not pre-exist as the Son of God prior to His becoming human as the Son of Man, then He could not be the eternal God.

———— ❧ ————

If Jesus came into existence only at His physical birth in Bethlehem, then He was not a part of the eternal triune Godhead, and could not have been the God-man with the necessary divinity to forgive sin (Mark 2:7; Luke 5:21) as the "God and Savior" (Titus 2:13) of mankind.

But because He was eternally pre-existent as the Son of God, the "Lord of glory" (I Cor. 2:8), in becoming fully human and functioning derivatively as a man, He could still say, "I and the Father are one" (John 10:30) — that, not merely a oneness of purpose or intent, but a oneness of divine essence, "true God and eternal life" (I John 5:20).

THE FATHER'S SENDING OF THE SON

In accord with the divine purposes expressive of the divine character of justice and grace, God the Father, in mutual determination with the Son and the Spirit, determined to send the Son on the redemptive mission to restore mankind to God's functional intent.

"God so loved the world that He gave His only begotten Son" (John 3:16). "He did not spare His own Son, but delivered Him up for us all" (Rom. 8:32), both in incarnation and atonement. Jesus Christ was "sent by God" (John 17:3) to do the will of God (John 6:38), to speak the words of God (John 3:34), and to do the works of God (John 14:10), in order that "the world might be saved" (John 3:17) and "the world might live through Him" (I John 4:9).

Jesus was continually conscious that He was sent by God the Father. "I proceeded forth and have come from God, . . . He sent Me" (John 8:42), Jesus told the Jewish authorities. He explained to His disciples that He had "come forth from God, and was going back to God" (John 13:3); "having came forth from the Father, and come into the world; I am leaving the world again, and going to the Father" (John 16:28). Jesus was forever conscious of His divine mission to man, as well as the necessity of man's "believing Him Whom God sent" (John 5:38; 6:29). In His intimate prayer wherein He foresaw the accomplishment of the divine work (John 17:4) in His own death, Jesus said, "I came forth from Thee, and they believed that Thou didst send Me" (John 17:8).

These verses, which indicate that God the Father sent God the Son on the redemptive and restorative mission to mankind, evidence that there is some kind of authoritative hierarchy within the Godhead. Such does not impinge upon the essential equality of Being between the three persons of the Godhead, but does reveal a differentiation of functional. Paul can thus state that "God is the head of Christ" (I Cor. 11:3), and that "the Son Himself will be subjected to the One Who subjected all things to Him" (I Cor. 15:28). Jesus Himself said, "The Father is greater than I" (John 14:28), but since that statement was uttered during His functional condescension as God-man on earth, it may not pertain to the functional placement of the members of the Godhead. Suffice it to say that God the Father was in a position to send God the Son to become a man.

———— ❧ ————

The sending of the Son was at the precise point in human history that God had determined. "In the fullness of time God sent forth His Son, born of a woman" (Gal. 4:4).

———— ❧ ————

All of the preparatory preliminaries had been accomplished in the Abrahamic promises and the Mosaic Law of the old covenant. The focal point of human history — when God sent His Son to become a man — is indeed divine intervention into the space/time context of humanity.

THE SELF-EMPTYING OF THE SON

God's sending of the Son to become a man was with the complete consensus of the Son to enact the divine mission. Being of one mind with God the Father, the Son was not a hesitant or reticent participant in the decisive endeavor to act on man's behalf. He was not forced by compulsion to assume the role and personification of the Messiah. Rather, He willingly and voluntarily condescended to waive the privileges of His divine function and subordinate Himself to God the Father in what is often referred to as His "humiliation."

Paul explained that in an attitude of humility Jesus "emptied Himself, taking the form of a bond-servant, being made in the likeness of men" (Phil. 2:5-7). The word that Paul employs for Jesus' self-emptying (*kenosis*) means "to counteract the function of" or "to lay aside the use of" something. The question must then be asked: "What did Jesus empty Himself of?"

Did Jesus divest Himself of His deity in order to become a man? No, for He could still say, "I and the Father are one" (John 10:30) in essence, as God.

Did Jesus lay aside His divine glory? No. The glory of God is in the expression of His character, and when the Word became flesh, John reports that "we beheld His glory, glory as of the only begotten of the Father" (John 1:14).

Did Jesus cast off some of the incommunicable attributes of His deity which were incompatible with humanity, such as the omni-attributes of omnipotence, omniscience or omnipresence? Some theologians have proposed such kenotic theories of deprivation and depotentiation, but such theories inevitably leave Jesus as less than God.

Since God is immutable, His nature and essence of Being cannot be changed or partitioned, for He is eternally, completely God, "the same yesterday and today and forever" (Heb. 13:8).

Jesus did not divest Himself of His complete and essential Being as God. His act of self-emptying *kenosis* was at the same time an expression of complete and full *plerosis*, for "the fullness of deity was dwelling in Him in bodily human form" (Col. 1:19; 2:9).

When considering the Christological formation of the Person of Jesus Christ, it is important to recognize the ontological factor of His Being as well as the operational factor of His function. Jesus could *be* God and *be* man at the same time, but it would not be possible for Jesus to behave or function as God and man at the same time. God is autonomous, independent and self-generating in His functional action. Man, on the other hand, is dependent, derivative and contingent in the receptivity of his function. The divine Son did not divest Himself of

His Being as God in any way, but did defer the independent exercise of His divine function in order to function dependently and derivatively as a man. His divine prerogative of direct and independent enactment of divine function was suspended in order to voluntarily subordinate Himself in human contingency and receptivity. This deferment does not dysfunctionalize deity, but allows deity to function in an indirect manner, as receptive man allows for the faithful expression of God's character of self-giving.

Such subordinated dependent function is illustrated in Paul's subsequent phrase indicating that Jesus "took the form of a bond-servant" (Phil 2:7). Indentured servants were perceived as functional tools to perform the master's desires. Jesus voluntarily assumed the dependency and humility of servanthood in order to serve the needs of mankind. Isaiah had prophesied that the Messiah would be a servant (Isa. 52:13) who would suffer (Isa. 53:3-12) on behalf of His people.

Willingly consenting to become the God-man, Jesus recognized that His function as a man was by the indirect receptivity of the works of God. "I do nothing of Myself, unless by the direct initiative and instigation of divine function," Jesus said repeatedly (John 5:19,30; 12:49; 14:10), but "the Father abiding in Me does His works" (John 14:10). Even the supernatural and miraculous manifestations evidenced during Jesus' ministry on earth were by the indirect functional receptivity of God's action. Peter declared in his first sermon on Pentecost that Jesus was a man "attested to you by God with miracles and wonders and signs which God performed through Him" (Acts 2:22).

The self-emptying of the Son in becoming a man did not divest or deprive Him of His eternal deity which cannot be altered. The self-emptying of the Son must be understood as the deferment of His direct divine function in order to allow for indirect divine function in "the man, Christ Jesus" (I Tim. 2:5), Who was faithfully receptive to such divine function in His behavior for every moment in time for thirty-three years.

The Conjoining of God and Man in the Person of Jesus Christ

The event of Christmas in theological terminology is referred to as the "incarnation," which means "in the flesh." God was enfleshed in humanity in the Person of Jesus Christ, born as a baby in Bethlehem. The apostle John begins his gospel narrative not with details of the physical birth of Jesus, but with the theological explanation that God, the Word (John 1:1), "became flesh and dwelt among us" (John 1:14). "The Word was manifested" (I John 2:1,2), "revealed in the flesh" (I Tim. 3:16), and the importance of such was explained by John when he wrote in his epistle that anyone "who confesses that Jesus Christ has come in the flesh is of God" (I John 4:2,3).

The One Who "existed in the form of God" was "made in the likeness of men, and found in appearance as a man" (Phil. 2:7,8). He "partook of flesh and blood" (Heb. 2:14), and "dwelt (literally, "tabernacled" by setting up His physical tent) among men" (John 1:14).

Paul's statement that "God sent His Son in the likeness of sinful flesh" (Rom. 8:3) must be carefully explained to avoid attributing any intrinsic or behavioral sinfulness to the Person and work of the sinless Savior. All "flesh," in the sense of humanity, is comprised in a sinful condition in spiritual solidarity with the choice that Adam made as the representative man (cf. Rom. 5:12-19). In such a collective condition all humanity can be described as "sinful flesh." The Son of God partook fully and completely of humanity with its tri-fold physical, psychological and spiritual capacities, but the "likeness of sinful flesh" is explained in that He was "unlike" fallen humanity because He did not partake of spiritual depravity and thus did not develop "flesh" patterns from prior selfish and sinful behavior. Though Jesus was fully human, humanness by definition is not necessarily inclusive of sinfulness, though it has been identified by its expression of such since the Fall.

Jesus, as God, became at the same time, fully man. How can this be accomplished, since attributes of divinity and humanity seem to be incompatible? It is admittedly inexplicable, for such a union of God and man creates paradoxical antinomies which are beyond human comprehension. But Christian theologians have spent centuries attempting to explain to the best of their finite understanding how God could be conjoined with man, deity with humanity, eternal with temporal, infinite with finite, spirit with physicality, for such is the essence of the divinely revealed incarnation of Jesus.

The Son of God became the God-man, Jesus Christ; a theanthropic person (*theos* being the Greek word for God, and *anthropos* being the Greek word for man). He was not a hybrid, nor homogenized by the absorption of either form of being (deity or humanity) into the other in subsumation or subsumption. His divinity did not merely employ His humanity as a container in adoptionistic instrumentalism, nor did His humanity simply consciously assume the mantle of Messianic divinity. His was a genuine and substantial union of divine and human in a singular personification of one real person, described by theologians as a *homoousion* oneness of being in "hypostatic union," i.e., standing united as one person.

Needless to say, the imprecision of explanation has allowed for numerous Christological variations and controversies throughout the history of Christian thought. The Docetists denied that Jesus was really human, claiming that He only appeared (*dokein*) to be human with a phantom-like, illusory body. The Ebionites denied that Jesus was divine, claiming that He was simply the natural son of Joseph and Mary who assumed and adopted the "Son of God" title at His baptism. The Arians denied that Jesus was eternally God, claiming that Jesus was created by God prior to the creation of the world. The Apollinarians questioned the deity of Christ, claiming that Jesus had a human body and soul but was invested with the divine *Logos* to replace His human spirit. The Nestorians posited that Jesus was really two persons in one, with a schizoid dual-personality in sympathetic union with one another. The Eutychians claimed that the divine and human substances were merged to form a third compound nature that was not really divine or human. Such variations and controversies of explaining how Jesus could be the God-man continue to this day.

A contemporary theological discussion of the Christological conjunction of God and man in Jesus Christ centers on the incarnational statement of John that "the Word became flesh" (John 1:14). How are we to interpret the word "flesh"? Does this mean that Jesus assumed the human physicality and tangibility of an individual human being in a physical body? Or can this be interpreted inclusively to imply that the divine Word assumed humanity at large, even to the extent that He subsumed humanity into Himself? If the latter interpretation is accepted, and the statement "the Word became flesh" is understood to mean that "God became man," this raises additional questions. Does this impinge upon the immutability of God by indicating that God became something He was not before, i.e., humanity? Is the nature of God thus changed? Is it legitimate, therefore, to refer to "the humanity of God"? In such an eternal union of God and man, is Jesus forever human? If so, does the eternal humanity of Jesus indwell the humanity of the Christian? Does the inclusive divine assumption of humanity necessarily imply the inclusive universalism of Christ's efficacy? Such questions should make us cautious of an overly inclusive interpretation that changes the biblical statement of "the Word became flesh" into "God became man."

THE THEOLOGICAL PURPOSE OF THE INCARNATION

God's purpose in the conjoining of His Son with man in the enfleshed Person of Jesus Christ was to reveal Himself to mankind in order to redeem men and restore them to His created intent. Jesus Christ, as "the visible image" of the invisible God (cf. II Cor. 4:4; Col. 1:15), revealed God as no one other than the "only begotten Son" could do. He revealed God (Matt. 11:27) and explained Him (John 1:18) so completely and efficaciously that Jesus could say, "From now on you know Him and have seen Him" (John 14:7).

The self-revelation of God in the incarnation of the Son revealed that God had not given up on man. In the action of His grace God revealed His love (John 3:16; I John 4:8,16) in His willingness to give His only begotten Son to become a man and die for men (Rom. 5:8) in vicarious assumption of the consequences of men's sin. The incarnation and the

47

atonement are inseparably linked. Jesus came to die! "The Son of Man came to give His life as a ransom for all" (Matt. 20:28; Mark 10:45; I Tim. 2:6). "Being found in appearance as a man, He humbled Himself by becoming obedient unto death, even death on a cross" (Phil. 2:8). "He partook of flesh and blood, that through death He might render powerless him who had the power of death, that is, the devil" (Heb. 2:14). The teleological purpose of the incarnation is that "God was in Christ reconciling the world to Himself" (II Cor. 5:19) as Mediator (I Tim. 2:5) and Savior (Luke 2:11; John 4:42; Titus 2:13; 3:6; I John 4:14).

———————— ẽ ————————

God wanted to restore man to His created intent by offering a new creation by His Word whereby His life was again invested in man to be expressed through man unto His own glory.

———————— ẽ ————————

There was no other way to effect such and maintain divine justice except that the God-man — One Who was man, capable of experiencing the death consequences; and One Who was God, capable of forgiving sin — would assume the conjunction of deity and humanity in one person in order to redeem, heal and restore the human race. That was why Gregory of Nazianzus (330-389 A.D.) explained that "the unassumed is the unhealed."

But these very features of God's self-revelation and self-giving in the Son are at the same time the stumbling blocks of reactive offense that natural men have towards the incarnation and crucifixion of Jesus Christ. An innocuous baby in a manger with ethereal angels, idyllic shepherds, and inquiring magi can be tolerated if recognized as containing some superstition. The death of a martyr on a Roman cross can be understood and accommodated by natural reasoning.

But the theological implications of the incarnation which assert that God acted supernaturally by entering into the space/time context of the world in the form of a man, this the natural man objects to, for in the sophistry of scientism modern man discounts the dimension of supernatural and miraculous divine action. That the incarnation could be God's unique and singular method of dealing with man's sin, and that the crucifixion should be the singular (Heb. 7:27; 9:28; 10:10) sinless (II Cor. 5:21; I John 3:5) sacrifice of redemptive efficacy for man's sin, this the natural man finds objectionable as contrary to his rationalistic premise of pluralistic means. That the introduction of divine life in a man by the incarnation of Jesus should be prototypical of the reinvestiture of God's life in all men (John 6:60; 14:6; I John 5:12) who would be receptive to Christ's resurrection-life, and that such divine life is indispensable to the proper function of derivative man, this is offensive to the natural man who regards himself to be adequate and competent for life in the philosophy of humanism. This explains why the theological implications of Christmas are received less frequently than the historical and cultural considerations.

Chapter 3

CHRISTMAS
Considered Celebrationally

The historical and theological considerations of Christmas gave rise to the celebration of Christmas among Christian peoples.

It is valid to question whether God ever intended that the birth of Jesus should be celebrated by Christians, for it is not scripturally ordained as are the ordinances of baptism and the Lord's Supper, nor referred to in the Bible as is the weekly Lord's Day observance (Acts 20:7; I Cor. 16:2; Rev. 1:10) on Sunday, the first day of each week. Our considerations of the celebration of Christmas are, therefore, not scripturally derived.

HISTORY OF RELIGIOUS CELEBRATION

There is little evidence of the celebration of the nativity or the incarnation prior to the fourth century. Irenaeus (c. 130-200 A.D.) and Tertullian (c. 170-220 A.D.) both omit any reference to the celebration of the birth of Christ from their lists of Christian feasts. Origen (c. 185-254 A.D.) noted that Christians celebrated only the weekly Sunday observance and the yearly Easter and Pentecostal feasts, going on to explain that Christians should not celebrate birthdays of saints and martyrs, including Jesus, only the date of their death. "Sinners alone, not saints, celebrate their birthday," Origen said.

During the fourth century many things changed as the church became linked with the Roman Empire after the conversion of Emperor Constantine in 323 A.D. Constantine's mother, St. Helena, went to Palestine in the mid-fourth century and claimed to have discovered the site of Jesus' birth in Bethlehem, whereupon a church building was constructed, remaining to this day as the oldest continuous church site in Christian history. In the Eastern Orthodox Church they began to celebrate Epiphany (meaning "manifestation" or "showing forth") on January 6, celebrating the birth of Jesus, the baptism of Jesus, and the arrival of the magi combined in one festival. The Western Roman church chose December 25 as its primary celebration of the birth of Christ, as documented by the decree of Pope Liberius in 354 A.D.

Gradually the Eastern and Western sections of the church began to merge their celebrations. In a sermon preached in 386 A.D., Chrysostom urged the Eastern church to celebrate the birth of Christ on December 25 as other portions of the church had so observed it for at least ten years. The Western church of Rome accepted January 6 as the celebration of Epiphany, celebrating the arrival of the magi on that date.

The celebration on December 25 was called *Nativitas Domini,* the Birth of the Lord, though Gregory of Nazianzus sought to change the name to Theophany (the manifestation of God) to correlate with Epiphany. The twelve days between December 25 and January 6 eventually became the "twelve days of Christmas," declared as such by the Second Council of Tours in 566 A.D. Roman Emperor

Theodosius was the first to declare *Nativitas Domini* as an official state holiday in 438 A.D. We observe, therefore, that the birth of Jesus has been celebrated by Christian people for over sixteen hundred years now.

In the fifth century, Perpetuus of Tours extended the celebration of *Nativitas Domini* to include an Advent preparation. Advent is derived from the Latin word *adventus*, meaning "to come." The Advent season was a time of liturgical worship in the four weeks preceding the celebration of Jesus' birth, wherein Christians were urged to remember the prophetic promises of the Messiah's coming, the preparation for such by John the Baptist, and the announcement of such by Zacharias. It was a time when Christians were urged to repent from drunkenness and promiscuity, to fast on Fridays, and to give generously. Advent season also recognized the expectation of the second advent of Jesus and the judgment of God.

The designation of the celebration of the birth of Jesus as "Christmas" is derived from the Old English words Cristes Maesse (first known reference in 1038) or Cristes-messe (first known reference in

1131). The meaning of both is "Christ Mass," referring to the three masses that the Catholic Church celebrated on December 25 to honor the birth of Jesus.

Nativity scenes with representations of Joseph, Mary and Jesus at the crèche (crib or cradle) were first employed by St. Francis of Assisi in 1223 as part of the midnight mass on Christmas Eve. Dramatic presentations and reenactments of the nativity then became common in the religious celebration of Christmas.

Objection to the religious celebration of Christmas by Christians has been voiced on several occasions and by various groups in Protestantism. In seventeenth century England during the time of Oliver Cromwell (1599-1658), the celebration of Christmas was banned. By an Act of Parliament in 1644 Christmas celebration was forbidden, shops were compelled to remain open, and plum puddings or mince pies were condemned as heathen. "Yuletide is fooltide" was one of their mottoes. The resulting conflict led to many deaths in Canterbury. This attitude was carried over to the settlements of the new country also, with Connecticut and

Massachusetts forbidding the celebration of Christmas.

RELIGIOUS CELEBRATION MERGED WITH SEASONAL AND CULTURAL CELEBRATION

Throughout the history of mankind, people have celebrated mid-winter festivals, and these were often scheduled around the winter solstice (the standing still of the sun before it began to rise and create longer days of sunlight). These were often times of feasting and revelry celebrating the year's harvest. Germanic tribes had mid-winter feasts celebrating the cold season when animals could be slaughtered and the meat would remain frozen, coinciding with sufficient time for their drinks to be fermented. The mid-winter celebration of *julblot* by the Scandinavians may be the origin of the Teutonic Yule feasts.

When the birth of Jesus first began to be celebrated in the fourth century, the Romans had their own mid-winter festivals. Roman religion was an amalgam of Greek mythology, animistic worship of the sun, and emperor worship. The feast of

56

Saturnalia was a raucous celebration from December 17 through 24. Roman Emperor Aurelian, in 247 A.D., had established December 25 as the feast of *sol invicti* (invincible sun), also referred to as *natalis invicti* (birth of the unconquerable) or *sol novus* (new sun), to celebrate when the sun began to conquer the long nights. The Roman calendar had not been adjusted, so the winter solstice occurred on December 25.

The Christians' calculation of the birth of Jesus on December 25 created a convenient opportunity for Constantine to replace and transfer the celebration of *sol invicti* or *natalis invicti* to *Nativitas Domini,* the celebration of the birth of the Lord. Transference of images could even be made, emphasizing Jesus as the victory of light overcoming the darkness of evil. The *sol novus* (new sun) was easily converted into celebration of the "sun of righteousness." As the Feast of the Sun became the Feast of the Son, church leaders emphasized that the naturalism of the solar cult was being replaced by the celebration of the supernaturalism of God sending His Son, Jesus.

Some Christians have been bothered by the realization of the transference of pagan rituals and their evolution into celebrations of the Christian religion. Study of human history reveals the inevitability of eclecticism and syncretism in the enculturation process of cultures and religions. Peoples from different places and different backgrounds will tend to blend and integrate their ideas and customs over time. Without a doubt there has been amalgamation as secular and non-Christian practices have been adapted into our Christmas celebrations.

When we objectively observe the traditions of our Christmas celebration in North America, it becomes obvious that there has been a merging of religious and cultural celebrations within our eclectic society. Many of what we might identify as cultural factors of Christmas celebration in North America have their origins in prior religious celebration. Some of our religious celebration is permeated with prior secular customs (for example, Santa Claus and Christmas trees). In fact, the origins of many of our Christmas customs and traditions are shrouded in speculative legends and fanciful interpretations.

What was the origin of Christmas carols, for example? Some would indicate that the first "carols" were the songs of the angels announcing the birth of Jesus to the shepherds near Bethlehem. A "carol" originally referred to a group dance accompanied by joyful song, and then gradually evolved into reference to the song itself. Some of our Christmas carols were derived from folk songs or traditional drinking songs, and early "caroling" festivities were performed by bands of men and boys going house to house demanding money or drink. Other carols were originally hymns of the church, some written by such great composers as Handel ("Joy to the World"), Bach ("How Brightly Beams the Morning Star") and Mendelssohn ("Hark, the Herald Angels Sing").

A carol that appears to be rather non-religious, "The Twelve Days of Christmas," is alleged by some to have been an underground catechism in the Catholic Church during the days when Christmas celebration was banned in England. Not only does it relate to the twelve days of Christmas from

December 25 to January 6, but some have interpreted hidden meanings as follows: The gifts of the "true love" are gifts from God to "me," every Christian. A partridge in a pear tree represents Jesus Who died on the tree of the cross. Two turtledoves represent the Old and New Testaments. Three French hens represent faith, hope and love. Four calling birds refer to the four gospels. Five gold rings are symbolic of the five books of Moses, the Pentateuch. Six geese a-laying indicate the six days of creation. Seven swans a-swimming refer to the seven gifts of the Holy Spirit. Eight maids a-milking represent the eight beatitudes. Nine ladies dancing refer to the nine fruit of the Spirit. Ten lords a-leaping indicate the Ten Commandments. Eleven pipers piping represent the eleven faithful disciples. And twelve drummers drumming are reputed to illustrate the twelve points of the Apostles' Creed. There is no known documentation to verify this interpretation.

What is the origin of the Christmas trees that we use in our Christmas celebrations today? Explanations are many and varied. Some have explained that evergreens were placed over the door during the Roman *Saturnalia* festival. Others would trace the origin to Druid tree worshippers. One legend indicates that a monk who went to Germany in the seventh century used the triangular shape of the fir tree to represent the Trinity of Father, Son and Holy Spirit.

St. Boniface is identified as the source of this representation in the eighth century. In the eleventh century there is evidence of evergreen trees being decorated with apples and bread to represent the "tree of life" and the "tree of the knowledge of good and evil" from Genesis 2 and 3, and called a "Paradise Tree." Evergreen trees were apparently hung upside down from the ceiling during the twelfth century as a symbol of Christianity, the fact that they remained ever green symbolizing eternal life.

Early references to evergreen trees being decorated during the Christmas celebration come from Riga in Latvia in 1510 and Strasbourg in France in 1604. Though some have attributed the introduction of Christmas trees to Martin Luther, there is no substantiation of such. General use of Christmas trees seems to go back to the end of the eighteenth century. Only in the middle of the twentieth century were artificial trees introduced.

Though some have repudiated the use of Christmas trees based on a passage from Jeremiah 10:3,4 in the King James Version of the Bible, where it reads that "the customs of the people are vain: for one cutteth a tree out of the forest . . . they deck it with silver and with gold; they fasten it with nails and with hammers, that it move not . . . ", this passage seems to deal with idols rather than Christmas trees, and it is obvious that God is not opposed to the use of trees in festivals for He established the Jewish Feast of Booths which utilized trees in religious celebration.

A recent phenomenon is the introduction of Chrismon trees. Chrismon is a combination word meaning "Christ monogram." Chrismon trees use only symbols of Christ as ornaments on the tree. All the ornament symbols, such as star, circle, triangle, cross, fish, butterfly, crown, chi-rho, I.H.S., alpha, omega, etc., are either white or gold, symbolizing the purity and value of Christ. This practice was initiated by The Lutheran Church of the Ascension in Danville, Virginia.

Other greenery and plants are also employed in our Christmas celebrations. Holly, for example, with its pointed leaves said to represent the thorns of Christ's crown, its perennial green said to represent eternal life, and its red berries interpreted to symbolize the blood Jesus shed for mankind. Mistletoe, which does not seem to have any religious background or symbolism, is attributed to the Celtic Druids who allegedly used it to cast spells, believing that if it was held over a woman's head she would be powerless to resist a man's advances.

The poinsettia, viewed by many as the "Christmas flower," is a relatively recent addition to our Christmas celebration. Joel Robert Poinsett (1799-1851) was a native of South Carolina who was appointed as the first American ambassador to Mexico (1825-1829). While in Mexico he saw a beautiful red flower in the Taxco del Alarcon region of southern Mexico. He brought some plants back to South Carolina and grew them in his greenhouse. It was later discovered that the Aztecs called the plant *cuetlaxochitl* and had extracted dyes for textiles and cosmetics from its bracts, as well as using the milky white sap, or latex, as a remedy for fevers. Those who wish to apply symbolism to all Christmas objects have explained that the shape of the flower can be seen as symbolic of the star of Bethlehem, the red colored leaves as a symbol of the blood of Christ, and the white flowers as representative of purity.

Many of the more liturgical churches have made an annual tradition of "The Hanging of the Greens" as they decorate their places of worship with the various plants and greenery used in contemporary Christmas celebration.

Advent wreaths have long been used by Christians in their celebration of the Advent preparation for Christmas. On a circle of greenery, four candles are placed; usually three purple candles and one pink candle. One candle is lit on each of the four Sundays prior to Christmas. The purple candles are lit on the "Sundays of abstinence" (Sundays 1, 2 and 4), and the pink candle is lit on the third Sunday of Advent, called Gaudete Sunday. A white candle is sometimes placed in the center of the wreath to be lit on Christmas Eve, and sometimes on each of the twelve days of Christmas.

The practice of using Advent calendars is also relatively recent, dating to the late nineteenth century. Little "doors" are marked for each day of the Advent season, and each "door" is opened on its respective day to reveal a scripture verse or a picture relating to Christ. The first known published Advent calendar was made available in Germany in 1903.

A predominant feature of our contemporary Christmas celebration in North America is the use of the tradition of Santa Claus. The concept of Santa Claus is definitely an amalgam of many customs and traditions from around the world. The primary historical and religious link is to St. Nicholas who was bishop of Myra in Asia Minor during the early fourth century. Born in the Lycian city of Patera in approximately 280 A.D., he was orphaned at an early age. He became a priest and bishop who was known for his anonymous deeds of kindness and giving, even begging for food and money to give to the poor. Tradition alleges that a particular nobleman had lost his fortune and did not have money for a dowry for his daughters. St. Nicholas went to the nobleman's house at night and anonymously threw a bag of gold through the window. In fact, he did so for all three daughters. One bag of gold is said to have landed in the girl's stocking which had been left to dry (possibly the origin of Christmas stockings). Nicholas was apparently present at the Council of Nicea. He died on December 6, which was proclaimed St. Nicholas feast day after Nicholas was sainted by the Roman Catholic Church. A basilica was built over his tomb in 540 A.D. He was regarded as the patron saint of children and gift-giving. In 1087 A.D. Italian merchants stole his body from its tomb and brought it to Bari in Italy, probably wanting to preserve it in their possession during the break between the Roman and Eastern Orthodox churches.

The evolution from St. Nicholas to Santa Claus involves the integration of many traditions. The Scandinavian god Odin was thought to visit earth to reward good and punish evil. Later there were legends of tiny creatures called *nisse,* similar to elves, and one of them, *Julenisse,* was portrayed with a red suit and long white beard, believed to come after Christmas Eve dinner and bring gifts. The Swedish gnome *Jultomten* was in the same basic tradition. The Germans had a tradition of a figure called "Winterman" who would come down from the mountains dressed in furs heralding winter. The

Dutch had a tradition of a character named *Sinterklaas* who rode across Holland filling children's shoes with food if they had been good, or a birch rod if they had been naughty. The British had a tradition of Father Christmas, which was similar to the French tradition of Péré Noel.

In the melting pot of Christmas tradition these were brought together in 1822 by Episcopalian minister Clement Clarke Moore when he published a fifty-six line poem entitled "A Visit from Saint Nicholas," now better known as " 'Twas the Night Before Christmas." The poem was written as an imaginative story to make his children laugh, but its later publication became a primary impetus for the characteristics now ascribed to Santa Claus.

The graphic image of Santa Claus as a rotund, robust, jovial, red-robed, white-bearded figure with a sack of toys is primarily attributable to American artist and political cartoonist Thomas Nast. He first drew Santa in 1863, dressed in the Stars and Stripes, and sympathetic with General Grant from the North. He continued to draw various illustrations of Santa Claus for over twenty years. Norman Rockwell drew an image of Santa Claus for the

Saturday Evening Post in 1931. But the image of Santa Claus that we are most familiar with today is that drawn by Haddon Sundblom, who seems to have drawn Santa in his own image for use as a major promotion of Coca Cola in 1931.

Though some Christians disparage and object to the use of the mythical character of Santa Claus in Christmas celebration, afraid that children will not be able to differentiate the myth of Santa Claus from the fact of Jesus, they fail to recognize that children need to pretend and imagine. That is why most children's literature is full of fictional fantasy and fairy-tales, fueling imagination and creativity. Soon enough the children will have to learn to adapt to the rationalistic objectivity of the adult world. Besides, Santa Claus is not a violent villain like so many children's heroes today. He is a mythical character who brings gifts for the enjoyment of the recipients, and that is consistent with the Christmas celebration.

The gift-giving tradition of our Christmas celebration has been traced back to God's so loving the world that He *gave* His only begotten Son (John 3:16). In addition, the magi brought gifts to Jesus of gold, frankincense and myrrh, fit for a King. The tradition of St. Nicholas, the patron saint of gift-giving, also provides a precedent for Christmas gift-giving.

Several food items have become part of our Christmas customs. Gingerbread first became available in Europe after the eleventh century when the Crusaders returned from the Middle East bringing a new spice, ginger. Many varieties of gingerbread were made in Europe and particularly for the feasting at Christmas, the practice later being brought to North America. Eggnog is a North American concoction inspired by the French drink *Lait de Poule*, which was a mixture of egg yolks, milk and sugar, to which Americans added various liquors, usually rum or brandy.

Christmas candy canes have several theories of origin. The choirmaster of the Cologne Cathedral in Cologne, Germany is said to have bent sticks of white candy into the shape of a cane to represent a shepherd's staff in the seventeenth century. Some date the origin of the candy cane to a Christian confectioner in England during the latter part of the eighteenth century. The most popular explanation seems to trace the candy cane to a confectioner in Indiana near the beginning of the twentieth century. The symbolism of the candy cane is explained by many as the flavor of peppermint which is similar to Hyssop, used in the Old Testament for purification and sacrifice. The white rock candy is said to represent the purity of Jesus Christ, the Rock. The shape of a shepherd's staff can also be turned upside down to form the letter "J" for Jesus. The large red stripe is alleged to illustrate the blood of Jesus, and the three small red stripes are reputed to indicate either the stripes of Jesus' suffering or the Trinity.

The first Christmas cards known to have been published in North America were published by Louis Prang of Boston in 1873. They bore images of Santa Claus.

What we see in these explanations of contemporary Christmas customs is a merging of religious, cultural and seasonal traditions from many countries over many centuries. The seasonal holiday of Christmas celebration in Western society today is a cultural phenomenon that must be accepted as such. It should be obvious that many features of the North American celebration of

Christmas are not as meaningful in other cultures.
As many of our traditions arise from the northern
climes of Western civilization, the images of a
"white Christmas," "winter wonderland," sleigh-
bells, "jingle bells," and snowmen mean very little to
those who celebrate Christmas in the southern
hemisphere or in equatorial regions, which comprise
a large part of the world's population. The pluralism
of our society also demands that we recognize that
peoples of other religions may adopt and adapt the
cultural features of the Christmas season without
accepting the Christian message of Jesus Christ as
Savior and Lord.

Observations on Christmas Celebration

The mixed amalgamation of our Christmas
celebration with traditions derived from pagan and
secular sources does not imply that participation in
the seasonal celebration necessarily involves
conforming to pagan practices of the past or
worshipping pagan gods. Though the celebration of
Nativitas Domini in the Roman church served as a
convenient replacement of the Roman celebration of

71

sol invicti on December 25, this was not just a
transference of emphasis, and the celebration of
Christmas does not owe its origin to the Roman
Saturnalia celebration as often alleged. The date of
December 25 is not defiled because it was previously
used for non-Christian celebrations, for defilement is
not attached to days, events or places, but pertains
to character contrary to God.

Those who repudiate the celebration of
Christmas are often religious purists who attempt to
establish their own spirituality and piety by rejecting
as unscriptural, worldly and non-Christian anything
that does not have explicit biblical mention. In their
sanctimonious and pious separationism they fail to
recognize the inconsistency in their utilization of
other cultural concepts and technological devices.

Claiming that much of the festivity and
commercialization of the season is "not the
celebration of Christmas, but the desecration of
Christmas," some have urged that people should
"remember the reason for the season," and have
appealed that we should "not take Christ out of
Christmas." Not that Christ could be taken out of
Christmas, for it is inherent in the name of the

holiday, which will not likely be changed to "Winter Gift Day."

While some Christians are repudiating the celebration of Christmas altogether, there are other Christians who are demanding the right to celebrate Christmas in the public display of Christmas symbols that explicitly refer to Jesus Christ. Legal battles have been fought over the civil right to display nativity scenes in public places, and to sing carols that refer to the birth and theology of Jesus in school programs. Little do we recognize the extent of the freedom that has been afforded to Christianity in our culture.

May we continue to extend the freedom to every man to worship and celebrate as he chooses. Christians themselves are free to celebrate Christmas or refrain from doing so, for Paul explained that "one man esteems one day above another; another esteems every day alike. Let every man be fully persuaded in his own mind" (Rom. 14:5,6).

Perhaps of greater concern should be the character and attitude displayed by Christians during the Christmas season. Many Christians are fighting their way through crowded department stores, grumbling about the crowds and the prices, fretting about their credit card balances, and are generally "bent out of shape" by the holiday hassles. In so doing they are denying the reality of Christmas by exhibiting character and attitude that is contrary to the character of Christ.

If we want people to know
"the real meaning of Christmas,"
then the character of Christ's life must be
lived out in our behavior during
the Christmas season,
as well as every other time of the year.

There is no doubt that some features of our cultural celebration of Christmas have been misused and abused. People drink too much; they eat too much; they spend too much; they give for wrong reasons. But they do that all year long too — and we cannot check out of life or repudiate our culture. Everything that God has made has been misused and abused — natural resources, sexuality, family relationships, etc. Just because they have been misused and abused does not mean we deny their validity or seek to dispense with them.

We may object to the self-indulgent merry-making, revelry and intoxication. We may regret the crass commercialism and greedy materialism. We may be incensed at the orchestrated shortages of particularly popular toys that artificially drive up the prices, extorting and gouging parents whose children desire and request such. But we must not fall prey to Ebenezer Scrooge's attitude of cynicism and criticism, which seeks to throw wet towels of disparagement on the entire celebration of Christmas. "Don't be a Scrooge!"

The gift-giving tradition of the Christmas season can indeed be perverted by social pressures and expectations of reciprocity. But recognizing that "God so loved the world that He gave His only begotten Son" (John 3:16), and that by His grace "He continues to give us all good things" (Rom. 8:32), Christians are to allow the givingness of God's indwelling character to continue to motivate their giving, believing that "it is more blessed to give than to receive" (Acts 20:35).

Christians can and will seek their own forms and patterns of worship in order to recognize the "worth-ship" of Jesus Christ, whether in December or any other time of the year. Some have sought to remember the birth of Jesus by baking a birthday cake and singing "Happy Birthday" to Jesus. The use of Chrismon trees in some churches emphasizes the theological symbols of the Person and work of Jesus Christ.

However we choose to remember the meaning of Christmas, we should not reject the seasonal and cultural emphasis. Christianity does not seek to divorce people from their culture, nor to destroy people's culture. Nor does it seek to escape or insulate itself from culture in the protectionism of a Christian ghetto.

——————— ❧ ———————

Our objective is to introduce Jesus Christ as the meaning to life in the midst of the culture.

——————— ❧ ———————

We should appreciate the cultural enhancement that is our heritage by way of Christmas celebration.

Would we not be the poorer without the enriched treasure of music, art, literature and theatre that creatively express the Christmas reality? For example: Milton's *Ode to the Nativity*, Dickens' *Christmas Carol*, Bach's *Christmas Oratorio*, Handel's *Messiah*, Raphael's *Alba Madonna*, Tschaikovsky's *Nutcracker Suite*, etc. Would we want to forfeit Mendelssohn's carol "Hark, the Herald Angels Sing" or Grüber's "Silent Night"?

There are so many positive and beautiful features of the cultural celebration of Christmas — the lights, the sounds, the fragrances, the tastes of specially prepared foods. It is a time of family gatherings and reunions, of Christmas parties and banquets, of Christmas bonuses to express gratitude for a job well done, of Christmas specials on television, and Christmas music broadcast throughout the stores and over the airwaves. Is this to be rejected?

Rather, the culture of Christmas provides a platform for explaining the foundational meaning of Christmas in history, theology and experience. In like manner as the people of Israel constructed memorials so that when their children asked, "What do these mean?" they could respond by explaining what God had done (Joshua 4:1-7), so when our children or neighbors see the symbols of the Christmas celebration and ask the same question, "What do these mean?" we can explain what God has done in His Son, Jesus Christ.

It is unfortunate that some Christians have been more concerned with correct belief and ritual than with celebrating what God has provided in His Son and providentially arranged in their culture. They have been more admonitory than celebratory. It is time to exercise our Christian freedom and enjoy and celebrate the Christmas season.

Chapter 4

CHRISTMAS
Considered Personally

The historical and theological foundations of
Christmas are essential, lest it be relegated to
mythical memories or subjective flights of fancy.
But, on the other hand, the phenomenon of
Christmas is more than historical remembrance,
theological formulations of doctrine, and an
amalgamated cultural celebration.

Christianity is more than an historical society to
remember events such as the birth of Jesus Christ.
Christianity is more than a theological society to
ponder the ideological implications and
interpretations of the events and teaching of Jesus
Christ. Christianity is more than just the "reason for
the season" of Christmas or Easter.

If the focal point of Christmas is just an historical event of the birth of a baby boy in Bethlehem, even though it was a divinely orchestrated historical event whereby God intervened in human history taking the form of a man, then it remains but a static event of yesteryear — a solitary, isolated event of peculiar interest to those inclined toward the recollection of the trivia of past events. The religious remembrance of such historical events and theological facts can obviously become its own collective entity. The celebration of Christmas with its cumulative customs and traditions can become a self-perpetuating phenomenon in its own right, with ever-increasing cultural accretions. The Yule log continues to roll downhill, gaining momentum and size as it rolls.

But the dynamism of Christmas is not just in a perpetuated celebratory season. The dynamic of Christmas is in the continuing divine action of incarnation, analogous to the singular action of the Son of God becoming enfleshed in human form in the "man, Christ Jesus" (Acts 2:22; I Tim. 2:5). The abiding reality of Christmas is sustained only by the

personal and spiritual experience of Christmas in
human hearts.

THE TYPE AND PROTOTYPE OF BIRTH AND INCARNATION

The singular, historical event of Jesus' birth
pointed beyond itself. Even the historical narratives
of Jesus' birth as recorded in the gospels of Matthew
and Luke indicate that His coming was for a
purpose beyond Himself, as Savior (Matt. 1:21; Luke
1:31; 2:11), Messiah (Matt. 2:4; Luke 2:11) and Lord
(Luke 2:11) for all people (Luke 2:10) in a kingdom
that would have no end (Luke 1:33).

Despite the fact that traditional religion has
emphasized the events of Jesus' life and death as the
object of Christian faith, allowing such faith to be
conceived as but mental assent to historical data, or
adherence to theological ideas, principles, truths or
doctrines, the events of the past cannot save us or
grant life to succeeding generations. Only when the
divine One Who was functioning in those past
events becomes dynamically contemporaneous
within men in every age and ontologically present to

reenact the realities of those events does the past event become actualized in present and personal application.

The event of the nativital incarnation inevitably recedes into prior history; and if regarded only as history, Jesus, like all figures of history, is removed from the present scene and survives only as a recollection in the records of those who reported such, and as a picture in the minds of those who review such. In such case the Christic incarnation becomes but an intemporation, a temporary insertion into or intervention in historical time, a transient Theopany of an historical visit of God to man. Those in subsequent times can have no relational integration with One Who is thus separated from them in time and space.

If the incarnational birth of Jesus is to have contemporary import in successive generations of mankind, it must have dynamic extension in the experiential actualities of personal impact, rather than just recollected assertion in the philosophical and ideological constructs of propositional compact. It "must be interpreted in the 'existentialist' terms of the Biblical testimony rather than the 'essentialist' categories of Greek philosophy."₃

The One Who was born in incarnation must continue to live and allow for His similar birth in others. The One Who was raised from the dead in resurrection must continue to live to invest His life in others. The historic events of incarnation and resurrection must represent (re-present) the ontological reality of the life of Jesus Christ in the present as "type" and "prototype" of His birth and incarnation in all men.

The birth of Jesus was a "type" of spiritual birth for all men. A "type" is a pictorial representation within a physical or historical act of a coming spiritual reality. The Old Testament is full of "types" which pictorially prefigured what God was to do in the new covenant arrangement in His Son, Jesus Christ. Those "types" were fulfilled in their "antitype" by the Person and work of Jesus.

The historical "type" of Jesus' birth can be observed in His conception by the Holy Spirit, being a precursor of the spiritual birth whereby Christians are "born, not of perishable seed, but imperishable" (I Pet. 1:23). The physical birth of Jesus was a "type" of the spiritual birth wherein Christians are "born from above" (John 3:7), "born of the Spirit" (John 3:8), "born of God" (John 1:13; I John 3:9; 4:7; 5:1,4). The incarnation was a "type" of the enfleshment of God's life in those who allow "the life of Jesus to be manifested in their mortal flesh" (II Cor. 4:10,11).

The implementation of these prefiguring "types" required the completion of the Messianic mission wherein the Son accomplished what the Father had sent Him to do (John 17:4). The purpose of His incarnational advent was to "seek the lost" (Luke 19:10), "bring light into darkness" (John 12:46), "save the world" (John 12:47), "call sinners to repentance" (Matt. 9:13; Luke 5:32), and to bring "life more abundantly" (John 10:10) in Himself (John 14:6).

But the prerequisite to the availability of His saving life was the assumption of the death consequences of human sin, made possible by His having become a mortal man. Jesus was born to die! He explained that the purpose of His coming was to die (John 12:27), "to give His life a ransom for many" (Matt. 20:28; Mark 10:45). The words of an Appalachian carol express the wonderment of this instrumental objective, wherein the purpose of Christmas was the crucifixion:

> I wonder as I wander out under the sky,
> How Jesus the Savior, *did come for to die*
> For poor ord'nry people, like you and like I,
> I wonder as I wander out under the sky.

Jesus did not come simply or solely to die. The death of Jesus was but the remedial instrumental purpose, designed to allow for the ultimate purpose of living and bringing life to all men. But the diabolic death consequences of sin had to be taken, to satisfy the justice of God (cf. Gen. 2:17), so "Jesus partook of flesh and blood that through death He might render powerless him who has the power of death, that is, the devil" (Heb. 2:14). The Son of God appeared incarnate for that purpose, "that He might destroy the works of the devil" by vicariously taking death upon Himself on behalf of all men in order to overcome that death with His life.

The subsequent resurrection of Jesus was also a "type" of birth, though seldom recognized as such. Preparing His disciples for His death and resurrection, Jesus used an analogy of birth (John 16:20-22), explaining that "when a woman is in travail she has sorrow" (as the disciples would have at the time of His death), "but when she gives birth to a child, the anguish turns to joy" (just as the disciples would rejoice when they saw Jesus again after the resurrection). Even more explicit is Paul's explanation that the resurrection of Jesus from the dead was the fulfillment of the promise of God in the Messianic Psalm (Ps. 2:7), where God declares, "Thou art my Son; today I have begotten Thee" (Acts 13:32,33).

Not only was the resurrection of Jesus a "type" of birth, but it also served as the "prototype" of life out of death. The death consequences that Jesus incurred on the cross included not only physical death but the death of separation from God's life as a man (cf. Matt. 27:46). The divine life was restored within the spirit of the man, Jesus, by resurrection. Jesus thus serves as the "prototype," the "first-born (*prototokos*) from the dead" (Col. 1:18; Rev. 1:5), Who would become the "first-born (*prototokos*) among many brethren" (Rom. 8:29) who would in like manner be brought to spiritual life out of spiritual death, and the "first-fruits of those who sleep" (I Cor. 15:20,23) in resurrection.

We recognize again the necessary connection between the incarnation and the atonement (inclusive of the resurrection). The resurrection is the complement of the incarnation, the parallel counterpart whereby they serve as "type" and "prototype" of spiritual birth in the "bringing into being" of God's life in man. The Christmas and Easter celebrations remain inextricably conjoined, as the events they remember together prefigure the availability of God's life in man.

THE CHRISTIAN'S INITIAL PERSONAL EXPERIENCE OF BIRTH AND INCARNATION

Corresponding to the incarnation and resurrection of Jesus, and in fulfillment of the "type" and "prototype" of divine life being expressed in man, men in every age can receive the life of the risen Lord Jesus by faith.

———————— ❧ ————————

**From "before the foundation of the world"
(Eph. 1:4; Heb. 4:3) this was the intent of God,
to reinvest men with His own life,
and the incarnation and resurrection of Jesus
were enacted to effect such.**

———————— ❧ ————————

Jesus' birth as a "type" is fulfilled when God's divine life is received into and "brought into being" again in an individual person. Such spiritual regeneration is figuratively portrayed in the New Testament by the metaphorical analogy of spiritual birth. Jesus explained to Nicodemus, the Jewish teacher, that "unless one is born from above, he cannot see the kingdom of God" (John 3:3). Continuing, He explained that such a birth necessitates being "born of water (physically) and of the Spirit (spiritually) . . . and that which is born of the Spirit is spirit" (John 3:5,6).

The "prototype" of Jesus' resurrection from the dead is also integrally connected to such a spiritual birth, for Peter wrote that "God has caused us to be born again to a living hope through the resurrection of Jesus Christ from the dead" (I Pet. 1:3), being "born again . . . through the living and abiding Word of God" (I Pet. 1:23), i.e., the living presence and activity of the risen Lord Jesus. Passing out of spiritual death unto spiritual life (John 5:24; I John 3:14), the receptive individual is "raised to newness of life" (Rom. 6:4) in conformity with Christ's resurrection.

Though some have denigrated and caricatured the concept of being "born again" spiritually (usually because of abuses and misuses of the phrase by less than astute Christians), the reality of the experience of receiving Christ's life is nonetheless legitimate and real. Swiss theologian Emil Brunner has noted that "there must really take place in us something corresponding to what once happened in Bethlehem; a birth through the Holy Spirit."[4]

The connection of Jesus' historical birth and the spiritual new birth of Christians has long been noted in Christian poetry. Poet Angelus Silesius, whose real name was John Scheffler (1624-1677), wrote:

Though Christ a thousand times
In Bethlehem be born,
If He's not *born in you,*
Your soul is still forlorn.

John Wesley's depth of theological
understanding is evident in the carol "Hark, the
Herald Angels Sing," written in 1739.

Hail the heaven-born Prince of Peace,
Hail the sun of righteousness.
Light and life to all He brings,
Risen with healing in His wings;
Mild He lays His glory by,
Born that man no more may die;
Born to raise the sons of earth,
Born to give them second birth.
Come, desire of nations, come;
Fix in us Thy humble home;
Rise, the woman's conquering seed,
Bruise in us the serpent's head.
Adam's likeness now efface;
Stamp Thine image in its place,
Second Adam from above,
Reinstate us in Thy love.

More than a century later, in 1868, Phillips Brookes of Philadelphia wrote "O Little Town of Bethlehem."

How silently, how silently
The wondrous Gift is given!
So *God imparts to human hearts*
The blessing of His Heaven.
No ear can hear His coming;
But in this world of sin,
Where meek souls will *receive Him still,*
The dear *Christ enters in.*
O Holy Child of Bethlehem
Descend on us we pray;
Cast out our sin and *enter in,* —
Be born in us today!
We hear the Christmas angels,
The great glad tidings tell —
O come to us, *abide in us,*
Our Lord *Emmanuel.*

The divine objective of the nativital incarnation was the spiritual regeneration of individuals throughout the entire human race.

———————— ॐ ————————

**Jesus was born in Bethlehem, so that
He could be born again in us.**

———————— ॐ ————————

It is important to note, though, that regenerative "new birth" is not an exact equivalent to the birth of Jesus in Bethlehem. Rather, our being spiritually "born of God" is analogous to the physical birth of Jesus delivered from the womb of Mary. Whereas in Jesus "the Word became flesh" as the God-man to function as mediatorial Messiah and Savior, Christians do not become God-men in the same sense, nor can they serve in the singularity of His Messianic function.

In analogous parallelism Christians do, however, become indwelt by the life of God (I John 4:15). We become "sons of God" (Gal. 3:26) and "children of God" (John 1:12; Rom. 8:16) in personal relationship with God as Father (Rom. 8:15). We become "partakers of the divine nature" (II Pet. 1:4) as the "Spirit of God dwells in us" (Rom. 8:16). We assume a new spiritual identity as "Christians" (Acts 11:26; 26:28), Christ-ones, being "partakers of

92

Christ" (Heb. 3:14) in spiritual union with Christ (I Cor. 6:17), participating in the mystery of "Christ in us, the hope of glory" (Col. 1:26,27).

The very life that was enfleshed in the historical Jesus is "brought into being" regeneratively in the Christian, and is incorporated into our innermost being, our spirit, our identity, our nature, to the extent that it can be said that "Christ is our life" (Col. 3:4). Jesus is not just a past pioneer and pattern, an exemplary model of how life should be lived. Nor is He merely the promise of life in the future for the Christian. Jesus is not just the medium and conveyer of the substance of spiritual life in the present, but He is in Himself "the way, the truth and the life" (John 14:6), the modality, reality and vitality of God in the Christian. As "the resurrection and the life" (John 11:25), the dynamic eternality of Jesus' resurrection-life becomes operative in the Christian.

Another unknown poet has expressed this truth:

I know not how that Bethlehem's Babe
Could in the Godhead be;
I only know the Manger Child
Has brought God's life to me!

The Christian's initial personal experience of spiritual birth and incarnation, in the receipt of the life of Jesus into himself, is analogous to Jesus' physical birth and incarnation in Bethlehem. Our regeneration and spiritual birth is an antitypical fulfillment of the "type" of Jesus' birth.

THE CONTINUING PERSONAL EXPRESSION OF INCARNATION

It will be instructive at this point to provide an historical review of God's dealings with man, in order to recall the logical contingencies, the historical connections, and the teleological purpose of the Creator's actions referent to man, the creature.

God's intent for man from the beginning of the original creation, as recorded in Genesis, was that man should express His character in a manner that no other part of the creation could do. Breathing His Spirit into man (Gen. 2:7), God provided His own presence in the spirit of man in order to visibly image (Gen. 1:26,27) His character in the behavior of the creature. Such exhibition and manifestation of His character was the incarnating and "fleshing out" of an invisible God in the visible expression of man, unto His own glory (Isa. 43:7).

When man's Fall into sin (Gen. 3:1-7) rendered void this indwelling arrangement for the incarnational expression of God's character, and God withdrew His presence in man, even so, it was God's loving and gracious intent to restore man to His created incarnational intent by His Son.

The natal incarnation of the Son of God, in the form of a man, allowed that mortal man, Jesus, to assume the death consequences of man's sin. But only by the entire living enfleshment of God's character in a man for every moment in time for thirty-three years could Jesus serve as the perfect and sinless sacrifice Who would substitutionally and vicariously represent all men in Himself. As that sinless One Who could not be held in death's power, He was triumphantly raised from the dead in incarnational resurrection with the power to provide His divine life to those for whom He had died. Those individuals willing to exercise their freedom of choice in reception of His life can thus be incarnationally regenerated or "born from above" with His resurrection-life, and that for the purpose of incarnationally manifesting the character of God visibly in man once again, to the glory of God.

_____ 🍎 _____

**The incarnational birth of Jesus,
the incarnational life of Jesus,
the incarnational resurrection of Jesus —
these all serve to provide for the regenerational
incarnation of God in the Christian,
and the sanctificational incarnation of
Christ's life in Christian behavior.**

_____ 🍎 _____

The teleological objective of God in creation is brought full-circle as He restores man in the "new creation" (Gal. 6:16), allowing the Christian to become a "new creature" (II Cor. 5:17), a "new man" (Eph. 4:24; Col. 3:10), in the context of a "new covenant" (Heb. 8:8,13), for His own glorification. Mankind is, as it were, "re-genesised" as the individual is regeneratively "brought into being" again with the life of God incarnationally dwelling within, and functioning through, the believer for the fulfillment of God's purposes.

The Christological incarnation that is at the heart of Christmas was more than just a natal or nativital enfleshment of physical condition at the birth of Jesus. John reported that "the Word became flesh *and dwelt among us*" (John 1:14). The world beheld the living and functional enfleshment and incarnation of God's life and character manifested in human behavior, bringing perfect glory to Himself (John 1:17).

Jesus did not come just to be admired as a precious baby in a manger, or as an ideal specimen of incarnated humanity. He came to live out the perfect life of God in a man, in order to be the perfect sinless sacrifice which would be the remedial solution for the consequences of man's sin, and then to rise victorious out of death to give His life to those who would receive such by faith and continue in that receptivity to manifest the divine life and character incarnationally. The import and impact of Christ's complete incarnation in birth, life and resurrection was intended to go beyond the parameters of a singular human form within a particular historical period.

**The infinite, eternal God
continues to invest Himself
in the space/time context of humanity,
incarnating His character in Christian people.**

In like manner as Jesus allowed for the incarnating of God's character in human behavior, serving as the visible "image" of the invisible God (II Cor. 4:4; Col. 1:15), Christians are to allow for a continuing personal expression of divine incarnation — the living enfleshment of Jesus' life — in their behavior. When a Christian becomes a "new self" indwelt by the divine life of Jesus Christ, he is renewed to the "image" of the Creator (Col. 3:10), allowing for the visible manifestation of God's invisible character in all he does. The conditional means of such an incarnational expression in the man is, as it was in the life of Jesus, the abiding presence of God, allowed to do His works (John 14:10).

The triune God — Father (John 14:23; I John 4:15), Son (II Cor. 13:5; Col. 1:27) and Holy Spirit (II

Tim. 1:14; James 4:5) — abides in the Christian for the purpose of functioning incarnationally, as the Christian contingently derives all from the proviso and Person of God's divine power, by the receptivity of His activity in faith. "As we received Christ Jesus (in regeneration), so we walk in Him (in the Christian life)" (Col. 2:6) by the receptivity of His activity — by faith. As the vine derives all from the branch (John 15:1-8), so the Christian can do nothing (John 15:5) to generate character of himself, but must recognize that "his adequacy is of God" (II Cor. 3:5) for the incarnational expression of all character and ministry (Rom. 15:18).

The Christian life is not an imitation of Jesus' example. Nor is it the moralism of conforming to prescribed procedures of piety; not even the biblicism of "going by The Book." The Christian life is the incarnational enfleshment process of allowing God's divine life to be lived out in man; the life and character of Jesus Christ lived out in a Christian.

Paul explained that "it is no longer I who live, but Christ lives in me, and the *life that I now life in the flesh* I live by faith in the Son of God Who loved me and gave Himself up for me" (Gal. 2:20).

———————— ❦ ————————

**The incarnational enfleshment
of the Christian life is
"the life of Jesus manifested in our mortal flesh"
(II Cor. 4:10,11), as Christ is progressively
"formed in us" (Gal. 4:19).**

———————— ❦ ————————

The continuing incarnational expression of Christ's life and character in the Christian has sometimes been referred to as "the extension of the incarnation," but careful distinction must always be made between the Christological incarnation of Jesus' enfleshment in birth, life and resurrection, and the Christian incarnation of "fleshing out" the life of Christ in regeneration and sanctification. There are indeed analogous corollaries and integrated features, but the Christian is never deified or divinized as God, and never subsumed, replaced, or transformed into Christ by escaping or rising above his humanity. The distinction between Creator and creature, God and man, Christ and the Christian must always be maintained without any monistic merging or syncretistic fusion.

100

Neither is it wise to refer to the restoration of God's presence and function in man as a "reincarnation" of God's life, in light of the Platonic and oriental implications of the term. To refer to the Christian as a "contemporary incarnation" of the life of Christ would be the better use of terminology.

It must also be noted that the incarnational expression of God's invisible character in visible manifestation is accomplished not only individually in and through each Christian person, but is also evidenced collectively in the Church, the Body of Christ, as the corporate incarnation of the life and function of Jesus. This is sometimes referred to as the "ecclesiastical incarnation" of Christ.

Since we are considering in this chapter the personal implications of Christmas, allow me to be so presumptuous as to address you, the reader, personally:

When the angels announced to the shepherds, ". . . *for you* is born this day in the city of David, a child Who is the Savior, Christ the Lord" (Luke 2:11), the plural pronoun "you" need not be interpreted only of the shepherds, nor of the nation of Israel, but for *all* men — including you, dear reader. I invite you to personalize the *"for you"* to be inclusive of God's objective, to apply the implications of the incarnation to your own life, as the Savior and Lord Jesus Christ is available to live and be enfleshed in you.

It is not until we, as individuals, allow the Christmas reality to transpire within us personally, by the introduction and indwelling of the life of the risen Lord Jesus, that Christmas finds fullness of meaning. Then Christmas comes alive and is enacted every day, as Christ lives in us, as us, and through us.

I urge you, dear reader, to consider carefully what Christmas means to you.

CONCLUSION

What are the conclusions to be drawn from our study of the history and meaning of Christmas?

To emphasize the historical, theological and celebrational considerations of Christmas without experiencing the personal birth and incarnation of Christ is but to engage in religionism.

To emphasize the celebrational and seasonal holiday of Christmas without regard to its historical and theological foundations or personal experience amounts only to humanistic culturalism.

To emphasize the personal and spiritual experience of Christmas without due regard to the theological and historical considerations gives rise to interiorized mysticism.

It is only when we consider Christmas fully — with its foundational history, its formulated theology, its festivities of celebration, and its enfleshment of the life of Jesus Christ in human behavior — that we are able to understand the fullness of Christmas. Only when we allow the incarnation of Jesus to become an experiential reality in our lives, in accord with its background of history and meaning, can we understand the reality of Christmas.

Christmas comes alive — every day of the year! — as we allow Jesus to become the incarnate expression of divine character in our behavior, within our families, our workplace, our culture, and wherever we might be.

Endnotes

1   Bruce, F. F., *The New Testament Documents.*
    London: The Inter-Varsity Fellowship. 1966. pg.
    119.

2   Josephus, *The Works of Josephus: Complete and
    Unabridged. The Antiquities of the Jews.* Book 18,
    chapter 3, section 3. Peabody: Hendrickson
    Publishers, Inc. 1987. pg. 480.

3   Hendry, George, *The Gospel of the Incarnation.*
    Philadelphia: The Westminster Press. 1958. pg.
    139.

4   Brunner, Emil, *The Great Invitation and Other
    Sermons.* Sermon entitled "Until Christ be
    Formed in You." Philadelphia: The Westminster
    Press. 1955. pg. 147.

Made in the USA
Middletown, DE
09 January 2022

58289877R00064